Red Eyed Tı

Red Eyed Tree Frogs Practical Keeper's Guide.

Information on care, enclosure, feeding, health and breeding.

by

Melinda Murkett

Published by: IMB Publishing

Photo credit for some photos: Gerard Siatkowski and Robert Baldwin.

Table of Contents

Table of Contents

Foreword

The red-eyed tree frog, *Agalychnis callidryas*. Photo by Robert Baldwin.

Chances are you've seen a red-eyed tree frog plenty of times, even if you've never walked into a pet shop that carries exotic animals.

In addition to being among the most beautiful of all amphibians in the pet trade, red-eyed tree frogs are the most widely recognised: they routinely appear on magazine covers, advertisements, and even billboards.

Their bright red eyes, smooth green skin, and blue-orange markings make them the literal 'poster frogs' of the rainforests where they originate.

Red-eyed tree frogs hail from the lowland rainforests of Southern Mexico and Central America. They are arboreal and live in the thick forest canopies, which shelter them from predators and the hot midday sun.

If a predator does approach them while they are sleeping, their red eyes flash open, an action known as "startle colouration" that usually sends the would-be attacker scurrying away.

Although bright colours normally indicate that an amphibian is poisonous (for example, poison dart frogs), red-eyed tree frogs are completely harmless.

These beautiful animals have been kept as pets for a while, but until recently their popularity was waning because they did not thrive in captivity.

Now, with advanced knowledge of their husbandry requirements and access to gadgets that help replicate their natural environment, red-eyed tree frogs are enjoying a revival among exotic pet enthusiasts.

The information in these pages will guide you in choosing a red-eyed tree frog (or frogs, as they are distinctly communal), setting up a perfect habitat, feeding it properly, and even breeding if that is your intention.

Captive-bred red-eyed tree frogs appear to be much hardier than wild-caught specimens, and by making them available in the pet trade, the need to remove frogs from their rainforest homes will lessen.

Although this book is the result of dedicated research and tips from reputable pet shops and long-time frog keepers, I will also be a 'voice of experience' in sections. I am the proud owner of Dexter, a four-year-old male red-eyed tree frog who has given me a lot of joy as well as a few frights that are now humorous in retrospect.

If you are thinking about getting a red-eyed tree frog, welcome to the fascinating world of exotic animal care. If you already have one or have succumbed to 'frog math' and gotten several, I hope that the contents of this book will help you deepen your enjoyment of these fascinating and beautiful amphibians.

This guide has been written by one person, but several enthusiasts contributed advice, answers, and photographs, and they deserve to be acknowledged.

Robert Baldwin, manager of the Reptile Store in Hamilton, Ontario (www.reptilestore.ca) sold me my first red-eyed tree frog and made amphibian-keeping appear to be such an enjoyable challenge that my 'jungle room' has since expanded to include green tree frogs and a dwarf pixie frog. Rob took many of the photos that appear in this book and continues to provide insights, advice, and moral support when necessary.

Gerard Siatkowski is a veteran amphibian breeder who contributes regularly to the major frog forums, thereby letting newcomers and long-time keepers alike benefit from his wisdom. Gerard was gracious enough to answer my questions and let me use some of his truly stunning photographs.

Bruce Carr and Kristina Vacek also deserve a special mention. Although his primary business is in tarantulas, scorpions, and other invertebrates, Bruce introduced me to some pretty amazing frog species, such as the Amazon milk frog. Kristina is an established gecko breeder but her enthusiasm for all things amphibian inspired my own love for the hobby.

There are others who helped with this project both directly and indirectly. They are the hundreds, if not thousands, of red-eyed tree frog breeders and enthusiasts who post regularly to Internet forums such as frogforum.net and let others learn from their successes and mistakes. Their contribution to this nascent but growing hobby is deeply appreciated. Thank you all.

Chapter 1) What is a Red-Eyed Tree Frog?

Dexter, the author's red-eyed tree frog. Photo by Robert Baldwin.

A Quick Introduction to the Basics

Red-eyed tree frogs are arboreal amphibians with toe pads that enable them to climb tree branches and leaves. Their species name is *Agalychnis callidryas*. *Callidryas* derives from the Greek words *kallos*, which means 'beautiful', and *dryas*, or 'tree nymph'.

The red-eyed tree frog is a member of the *Hylidae* (which encompasses all true tree frogs) family and *Phyllomedusinae* (monkey frogs) subfamily, which has six major subdivisions and over forty recognized species. Its native habitat is the lush rainforests of Central America.

This brightly coloured frog, now hailed as the quintessential rainforest amphibian, makes an attractive and rewarding pet for those who are willing to meet its requirements in captivity.

Red-eyed tree frogs seldom exceed 3" (76mm) in length. Despite their relatively small size, they can jump great distances, a feat that has earned them the nickname of 'monkey frogs'.

Their colour and size can vary depending on country of origin. The smallest specimens are from Mexico and Guatemala, which is the northern border of their native region. These frogs also tend to have pale blue sides. The larger frogs come from Nicaragua, Costa Rica, eastern Panama, and other countries on the southern edge of their habitat. In addition to their greater size, frogs from these areas are distinguished by their darker blue flanks.

The typical red-eyed tree frog has bright red eyes, a smooth green body with yellow and blue side stripes, and bright orange feet and toes with well-rounded adhesive pads and partial webbing. Some have white spots on their backs. Young frogs are brown and turn their characteristic bright green upon maturity. There are also different colour morphs, such as albino, pink, and purple, which will be featured in later pages.

Because they rely on camouflage for protection, red-eyed tree frogs change their colour in accordance with the day-night cycle. During the day, the dorsum (back) is bright green, but the colour deepens as night falls.

Behaviour

Like most frogs, red-eyed tree frogs are nocturnal. In the wild, they sleep all day under leaves and other foliage. When not breeding, they can usually be found in trees, preferring heights of 10 metres or higher.

At night their colours bloom and they go hunting, seeking insect prey among the thick leaves of the forest canopy. As soon as daylight approaches, the frogs find the nearest safe and shady spot and settle down for the day.

Red-eyed tree frogs are carnivorous, and eat flies, crickets, moths, butterflies, and other insects. They'll even eat small invertebrates and other frogs: something to bear in mind if you're thinking about giving your frog a roommate.

During the night time hours of the rainy season (approximately May to December) in their natural environment, male red-eyed tree frogs huddle in vegetation located near flooded ditches, ponds, and fields and call for mates. They perch at heights anywhere from one to five metres off the ground. Some nights you can hear hundreds of males calling!

Why Do They Have Such Bright Red Eyes?

During the day, the brightest parts of a red-eyed tree frog are hidden away in its state of huddled sleep. All you see is the smooth green back, blending in nicely with the surrounding foliage. If the frog is startled awake, however, its traffic-light eyes fly open and it changes position, revealing its brightly coloured side stripes.

So why does this species have such brilliant eyes? There are different theories, but the dominant one is that the sudden flash of red is a form of protection. Referred to as "startle colouration", it is believed that the abrupt appearance of such a vibrant colour startles the frog's natural predators and makes them hesitate long enough for the frog to escape.

Other animals use this trick. Certain moths and butterflies, such as the *Bicyclus anynana*, have coloured spots on their hind wings that resemble huge eyes. Like the red-eyed tree frog, they hide during the daylight hours. But if startled or attacked, they extend their front wings, revealing what looks like a pair of huge eyes and surprising the interloper long enough to escape.

The red-eyed tree frog's huge eyes actually have a third eyelid called a nictitating membrane, which offers extra protection. Since the frog's ability to survive in its native habitat hinges to a certain extent on keeping its eyes in shape, this is a useful –not to mention life-saving- feature.

Frog Anatomy 101

The body of a frog has three primary segments: the head, a short neck, and a torso. It's head movement is limited by its short and rigid neck. The torso encompasses a single body cavity known as the coelom, which holds the frog's internal organs.

Frogs have the same organs and organ systems as humans: heart, lungs, intestinal tract, kidneys, stomach, spleen, liver, pancreas, the gall bladder, and more. But in certain respect's the frog's anatomy is simpler: it does not have ribs or a diaphragm, and it has fewer bones.

A frog's skin is made up of two layers: an outer epidermis and an inner dermis. The skin is actually a breathing organ: frogs take in oxygen through it. (They also have a pair of lungs, which let them breathe when on land). Frogs can also detect low-pitched sounds through their skin.

The frog's eyes, the mouth and nostrils are all examples of its external structures, which also include its webbed feet and the cloaca opening. Frogs do not have external ears.

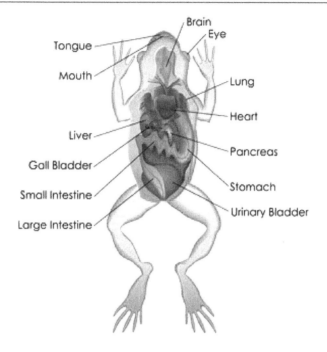

Overview of a frog's anatomy.

Frogs as Pets

During the past twenty years, frogs have become more popular in pet shops, even those that are considered more mainstream. The primary reason is that most species are low-maintenance and do not cost a lot to feed and house, unlike other exotics, which may require cage upgrades and eat expensive prey items such as mice and rats.

Tree frogs in general and the red-eyed tree frog in particular make stunning display animals. They love to climb and perch on branches, plants, and other cage decorations, and the males of some species will serenade the room during breeding season. Frogs, along with geckos, anoles, and chameleons, are taking centre stage in beautifully recreated vivaria.

13

Captive-bred specimens are available in pet shops and via breeders, which is good news. Commercial exploitation and lack of protective legislation have diminished the wild population of many animals now popular as pets, and the availability of a captive-bred population will lessen the need to remove red-eyed tree frogs from their rainforest homes.

In general, red-eyed frogs are undemanding and inexpensive to feed. They do, however, have certain environmental needs that could make them a challenge for novice keepers, but these are no longer impossible obstacles. Walk into any reptile-oriented pet shop and the shelves and aisles will be full of glass terrariums, fake and real plants, and artificial waterfalls and foggers.

Keeping these beautiful tree frogs successfully requires certain knowledge that used to only come with trial and error. Now, with frog keepers sharing their insights all over the Internet, there is a lot more data available, but the process can still be confusing and a little intimidating.

That's why this book was written: to make the process less 'mysterious'. You don't need to be a zoologist with a host of expensive climate-control equipment to keep your frog healthy and happy. These pages, which received a lot of input from experienced frog keepers, will tell you how to acclimatise your new pets, put together an enclosure that they will thrive in, feed them properly, and even breed them. It is a practical guide for those who want to join the growing ranks of those who keep this beautiful rainforest amphibian as a pet.

Chapter 2) Red-Eyed Tree Frogs as Pets

Dexter at night. Photo by Robert Baldwin

Before the mid-1980s, red-eyed tree frogs were rarely seen outside of the specialty pet trade. Then, according to Philippe de Vosjoli, Robert Mailloux, and Drew Ready, authors of *Popular Tree Frogs* (Advanced Vivarium Systems, 2005), U.S. importers started receiving hundreds of reptile and amphibian species from the Honduras and selling them to the general public.

These exotic new pets included forest chameleons, emerald swifts, palm salamanders, and red-eyed tree frogs. Herpetoculturists (those who keep amphibians and reptiles in captivity, usually for the purpose of breeding) eagerly brought them up and attempted to replicate their native environment. They weren't always successful.

As the decade drew to a close, all reptile shipments from the Honduras ceased. Then the red-eyed tree frogs that had been imported earlier started dying off due to neglect and ignorance about their husbandry needs. By 1990, only a few hundred remained in private collections throughout the country.

Now, fortunately for those of us who appreciate this exquisite amphibian, red-eyed tree frogs are finding their way back into exotic pet shops all over the world, thanks to new imports from Central America and, even better, successful captive breeding.

Owning a Red-Eyed Tree Frog: the Pros and Cons

Let's get the negative stuff out of the way first. Red-eyed tree frogs are not for everyone. They are nocturnal, so if you want a vibrantly coloured pet that is active during the day, a reed frog or poison dart frog would suit your purposes better.

Red-eyed tree frogs are also not especially interactive with their owners: if you want a pet that you can occasionally handle, go for a White's tree frog or an oriental fire-bellied toad instead. They also have precise temperature and humidity requirements that make them high-maintenance and not an ideal choice for the first-time amphibian-keeper.

Sounds daunting, doesn't it? So why did I buy one? And why should you?

Personally speaking, I don't need to touch or hold a pet in order to properly enjoy it. The first time I laid eyes on Dexter in my local pet shop, his beauty and grace moved me. Because red-eyed tree frogs need to be kept in conditions that replicate their original habitat, it was like beholding a piece of the rainforest in a compact glass cage.

I knew that caring for him would be a challenge, but during my twenty-plus years of pet ownership, I'd kept (and still keep) Goliath bird eater tarantulas that need controlled humidity to successfully malt and maintained a saltwater aquarium with zebra lionfish and aquacultured corals.

Dexter was, and continues to be, an easy and delightful undertaking compared to the above. Once his basic needs were understood and accommodated, he was no more difficult to take care of than my White's tree frog, Bumper, or my collection of New World tarantulas (also affectionately known as my 'pet rocks').

Once you have your red-eyed tree frog properly set up, it's cage or vivarium will command attention from visitors, act as a conversation piece, and be relaxing to behold, like a tank of gracefully swimming tropical fish. Your frog may even give you a few frights followed by hilarious closures: once Dexter escaped without my knowledge (my flatmate accidentally left the cage door ajar after feeding him), but he was promptly recaptured when a guest who came for dinner saw him sleeping on the television stand, thought he was a toy, and tried to pick him up. His eyes flew open, and the visitor's startled shouts brought me running.

Once she recovered from her shock, the visitor was fascinated by him, and is now the proud owner of three red-eyed tree frogs of her own.

Licensing

Red-eyed tree frogs, unlike some of their amphibian cousins, do not as a rule require a license to own them. However, countries like Australia have licensing requirements for some frog species and Hawaii makes importing Cuban tree frog a criminal offense, so it's a good idea to check your local regulations to see if there are any limitations on frog ownership.

Chapter 3) Where to Buy

Red-eyed tree frogs can be difficult to source locally, as they are not mainstream pets (yet!), but with a little effort, your search will pay off. They can be found at specialty pet shops and expos dedicated to the exotic pet trade. In some places a local breeder may have a selection of healthy, captive-bred specimens to choose from.

Red-eyed tree frogs can cost anywhere between $40 and $200 US (between £23 and £120), depending on the age of the animal and where you purchase your pet. Don't be afraid to shop around and compare prices until you find an option that fits your budget. And don't forget to factor in the cost of housing, food, and supplies such as heating, lighting, and cage decorations.

If you can afford it, consider getting more than one frog. Red-eyed tree frogs are communal and actually do better in a small group. If you can successfully mimic their native climate conditions and habitat, you may even be successful in breeding.

Red-eyed tree frogs are happier in small groups. © vitamin2b - Fotolia.com

Pet Stores

If you're lucky, your local pet shop will have at least one red-eyed tree frog in stock. But if the shop focuses on more conventional animal companions, like cats, birds, and fish, you may have to do a little travelling and research to find somewhere that specialises in reptiles and amphibians.

Here are some tips on choosing a good pet shop from which to purchase your frog and its supplies. Some of these suggestions hold true for selecting any retail outlet with which you wish to do business, while others are specific to the exotic pet trade:

- In good pet shops, you should be greeted within moments of your arrival, and asked if you require assistance or have any questions. Even if it is a weekend and the shop is busy, you should be acknowledged immediately.

- The shop should be clean, well lit, and adequately stocked with pet supplies. The aisles should be wide enough to walk through without tripping over merchandise, and all animal cages should be clean and free of broken or hazardous decorations.

- There should be no sick animals on display. Reputable shops keep all ailing animals away from public view, so they can recover in a stress-free environment.

- Ideally, there should be supporting literature such as guidebooks for all the animals they sell. The advent of the Internet and free online information has drastically reduced the number of books that pet shops carry, but a location that specialises in exotic animals should have a few publications by recognised experts or reputable breeders in stock.

- The best shops have the best interests of the animals first and foremost, and will not try to sell customers higher-ticket but totally unsuitable accessories and enclosures.

In general, smaller specialty locations tend to have more experienced and knowledgeable staff than the big chain shops or pet sections of large department stores. In my favourite shop, the manager actually breeds certain species of reptile, and individual staff members are enthusiastic about their favourite animals. One is a self-proclaimed "turtle nerd" and another one is a successful tarantula keeper.

If you find a shop that you like and feel you can trust but they don't have any red-eyed tree frogs in stock, see if they will order one for you. Most times, if the frogs are available from their supplier, they will be happy to oblige.

Exotic Pet Expos

Expos dedicated to the exotic pet trade and hobby are held all over the world. Vendors include breeders and sellers as well as suppliers. Expos usually have their own website, so visit it in advance and find out which breeders and / or companies will be exhibiting. I have yet to see an exotic pet expo that didn't have at least one vendor offering red-eyed tree frogs.

If you don't want to travel for nothing, make a note of all vendors whose company website indicates that they sell amphibians. Then e-mail them and find out if they'll be bringing any red-eyed tree frogs to the expo. Even if they weren't planning to, chances are they will if interest is expressed.

Breeders

Whenever possible, buy from a breeder. You will know everything about your frog's age and the health of its parents, which gives you a reasonable expectation of how long you will enjoy its company.

Since amphibian breeders tend to be dedicated hobbyists who take pride in their stock, you can be reasonably sure that the animal was raised in a healthy environment. Parasites, transit-related injuries, and other problems that beset wild-caught frogs are largely absent.

Try to buy from a breeder who is willing to provide you with customer references. If you are acquiring your first red-eyed tree frog, you want to be able to contact the breeder if you have questions or something worries you (Trust me, it will happen!). Past customers will be able to tell you how supportive and communicative the breeder is, as well as the quality of their livestock.

Common Pet Trade Acronyms

When you conduct online research, you will see certain acronyms next to species' names. Here are a few of them and what they mean.

CB: Captive-bred

WC: Wild-caught

J: Juvenile (recently morphed from froglet to frog)

F: Female

M: Male

For the first-time or novice frog keeper, captive-bred animals are the best choice. The chance of them carrying parasites is minimal and a good breeder would have raised them in a controlled environment conducive to good health. Gender doesn't really matter, unless you intend to eventually breed your pets.

Chapter 4) How to Choose a Healthy Pet

When you're looking for a healthy pet frog (and everyone is), nothing beats a captive-bred specimen. They are better adjusted to captivity than their wild-caught counterparts and much less likely to succumb to stress-induced complications. But if the only available options are wild-caught, there are steps you can to take to ensure that you get a healthy pet.

Visual Inspection

When selecting your frog, it is important to assess its condition and overall health. If the frog is wild-caught, it will have travelled a long way to reach the shop or seller; a gruelling process that leaves many animals stressed and in poor shape.

Take a minute to observe the frog or frogs. If a red-eyed tree frog perches on the glass walls of its enclosure or a tall piece of decor such as a plant or piece of cork bark, it's a promising sign of good health. Frogs that sit or huddle on the floor are probably stressed, a state caused by improper cage conditions.

Choose an animal that appears to have a healthy body weight. Then inspect it carefully for skin abrasions, swollen legs, or clouded eyes. The outlines of their bones should not be visible. Because wild-caught frogs are shipped in small containers, snout damage is not unusual, but it should not be extensive. If you see a frog with a badly damaged snout, recommend that the seller have it treated.

If faeces are visible in the enclosure, see if they look 'normal'. Watery or bloody faeces are definite signs of illness or some other physical problem.

Because red-eyed tree frogs are nocturnal, animals that are wide-awake during the day are probably ill or have something else wrong with them.

Wash your hands in clean water (no soap or hand sanitizer). Then, with the shop assistant or breeder's help, carefully hold the frog, keeping your hand inside the enclosure to prevent a steep fall if it jumps. The frog should be quite keen to get off your hand, and show it. If it sits limply, it is probably ill.

Colour Phases

Very few people get to see the alternate colour phases of the red-eyed tree frog. In addition to the bright green that everyone is familiar with, there are lutinos (albinos), xanthic (pale yellow with white eyes and black pupils), pinks (which have beady black eyes instead of the typical red) and purples, which also have dark eyes.

These colour morphs are usually available only at expos or via private breeders, and are more expensive than their bright green counterparts.

Red-eyed tree frog, lutino / albino phase. Photo by Gerard Siatkowski.

Pink red-eyed tree frog. Photo by Gerard Siatkowski

Purple red-eyed tree frog. Photo by Gerard Siatkowski

Distinguishing Between Males and Females

Sexing red-eyed tree frogs is fairly easy, as there is a substantial size difference between males and females. When mature, males average between 2 and 2 ½" (51 to 64mm) while females can reach 3" (76mm) in size. Males who are ready to breed also have brown nuptial 'pads' at the base of their hands.

Juveniles don't have a strong sexual dimorphism, although an experienced eye can detect the slightly truncated snout characteristic of females.

Mixed Company

Red-eyed tree frogs thrive in a communal environment: as long as that environment consists of others of the same species. If the inhabitants are of similar size, that is even better.

Rule number one: do not mix frogs and reptiles in the same enclosure or vivarium. I don't know of any vivarium-compatible reptile species that will not regard a red-eyed tree frog as a tasty but expensive meal.

I heard about one hobbyist who put a young red-eared slider turtle in with her two frogs. A few days later, she found that one of the frogs had some bite injuries. Although the animal recovered after the turtle had been re-housed elsewhere, it could have gone very badly, as broken skin can result in a parasite or fungus infestation.

Here are more things to bear in mind if you are thinking of mixing your frogs with other species:

- Amphibians can carry toxins in their skins that can harm other species. Korean fire-bellied toads (*Bombina orientalis*), for example, can poison other animals they are housed with.

- Fish are potential carriers of trematode worms, parasites that infiltrate their hosts and lay eggs. If a frog becomes infected, it won't display symptoms until it has passed the point where it can be helped.

- Some snail types (for example, ribeiroia snails) can carry parasites such as flatworms, which are known to cause deformities in amphibians. Since flatworms can also be dangerous to humans, why take any chances?

To keep things safe for your pets as well as yourself, group them only with other red-eyed tree frogs of comparable size.

The Tools of the Trade

Below is a list of recommended supplies. If you haven't purchased any of these items already, do so at the same time you buy your frog(s):

- 20-gallon glass tank

- Screen lid

- Real or fake plants (If you choose real plants, philodendrons and Pothos are great)

- Under-tank heating pad

- Ceramic heat emitter or heat lamp

- Lighting source

- Thermometer

- Humidity gauge

- Water bowl

- Vitamin / calcium powder

- Live crickets

- Cage decorations such as rocks, cork bark, or treated branches

- Misting sprayer

- Recommended substrate

Chapter 5) Bringing Your Red-Eyed Tree Frog Home

Quarantine

If you already have one or more red-eyed tree frogs, do not introduce newcomers to them right away. Opinions differ on how long the quarantine period should last, but if you wait sixty days, you will have covered all your precautionary bases.

Keeping new frogs separated from the main vivarium / enclosure like this allows you to observe them closely and detect illness before it becomes untreatable. The recommended quarantine period provides ample time for any viral, fungal, or bacterial infections to display their symptoms.

Create a 'quarantine tank' by placing the new frog in a tall glass or plastic enclosure with a screen top. Most experts recommend that the tank be at least 20 gallons: if you are quarantining multiple red-eyed tree frogs, follow a general rule of 5 gallons per frog, with a 20-gallon minimum.

Do not, however, quarantine multiple frogs in the same container unless they were living together at the time you purchased them.

These special-use tanks should be glass, not acrylic, to avoid grooves and scratches that could eventually harbour harmful bacteria. Glass is easier to clean and sterilise after the quarantined frog has been successfully introduced into the vivarium.

The same principle applies to decorations: do not use plastic objects that could be scratched and therefore compromised.

Line the bottom with paper towel and provide a good-sized water dish. Include some pieces of cork bark and at least one potted plant for the frog to climb and hide behind. Live plants are also great for elevating the relative humidity in the enclosure.

Put a dish of water in the enclosure, keeping it low enough that the frog can bathe in it to rehydrate itself.

During the winter or if the weather is unseasonably cool, adding a red incandescent bulb over a section of the tank will help stabilise temperatures. You can also use a heater pad designed for reptiles, as these pads tend to heat the air more evenly.

DO NOT improvise with a heating pad intended for humans, as the temperature range will be too hot for a frog.

If your new frog is wild-caught, it will need to be acclimated to help it adjust to its new surroundings. I know a hobbyist who has excellent success with stabilising imported frogs by keeping all of his new animals in a room with a cool-air humidifier. (De Vosjoli et al also recommend this, except in locations where the relative humidity is moderate to high). Avoid humidity levels of 85 and above.

Offer some prey items to the frog before leaving it for the night. Remove any uneaten prey the following morning and discard: do not offer the crickets / insects to your other frogs.

During Quarantine

When you check your frog each morning, count the crickets to make sure it is eating. If it is, examine its faeces for any sign of diarrhoea and other abnormalities. If you see anything that concerns you, contact a veterinarian.

Clean the paper towel on the floor of the enclosure every few days. To minimise stress, do this type of maintenance during the day, when the frog is sleeping. The water dish and cricket bowl (if you have one) should also be cleaned every day.

Your frog might not eat right away, especially if it is still adjusting to its new surroundings. As long as there is no evidence of illness, be patient and give the animal as much darkness and quiet as possible.

28

Find a small bowl to put the crickets in. When the frog is ready to start eating, it will approach the bowl of its own volition, drawn by the movement of the insects. It may take the frog a while to get used to eating from a bowl, but this is one of the best ways to feed it during the quarantine period, as you will be able to count the crickets in the morning and see how many have been consumed.

Any that have not been eaten can be returned to a cricket pen reserved exclusively for quarantined animals and be re-introduced the following evening.

If the frog appears to be dehydrated, mix a 1:10 pedialyte and distilled water solution and drip a little on its back a few times a day, while it is sleeping. Make sure the entire back area is covered while avoiding the facial area.

Many veteran keepers recommend this rehydration method because it allows the frog to be treated without having to handle it and create further stress.

If you do end up touching the frog and you have other amphibians to take care of, wash your hands in hot, soapy water after dealing with the quarantined pet. Rinse thoroughly, apply anti-bacterial hand sanitiser, and let it dry. Then rinse your hands in cold water.

Hand sanitiser is dangerous to frogs, so precautions must be taken to make sure any residue is gone before you deal with your other pets.

After Quarantine

After the quarantine period ends, you will need to sterilise the tank. Do the following:

- Purchase an eye dropper and set it aside for this purpose alone

- Pour water into a bucket and add 10 drops of bleach per gallon

- Scrub the tank with a soft-bristled brush and swirl the treated water about

- Let the water sit in the tank for 2-3 hours

- Rinse out with clean water.

After the tank has been rinsed clean, add more water and add in three tablespoons of table salt. Swirl it about, making sure that the salt touches the glass walls all the way to the top.

After letting it sit overnight, rinse at least twice to remove all traces of residual salt and bleach. Let the tank air-dry. Then mist it with a good anti-fungal spray before using it again.

To minimise the risk of infecting the wild amphibian population, dispose of all materials used in the quarantine tank (i.e. substrate) by placing them in a plastic bag, spraying the contents with a bleach solution, and tying the bag securely shut. Wash your hands thoroughly afterwards.

Handling

Frogs do not like being handled, although some species, such as the White's tree frog, appear to tolerate it. So keep handling to a bare minimum.

I have never actually picked up Dexter, although he's surprised me a few times by jumping on me. I made sure that he was returned to his cage as quickly and gently as possible.

Times may arise when you need to handle the frog, namely to dispense medicine or recapture an escapee. The best way is to cup the animal in both hands to prevent it from jumping and accidentally injuring itself.

If the frog does actually squirm free and make it to the floor, gather it up as quickly as possible and bathe it in distilled water before returning it to its enclosure.

It is important to remember that your red-eyed tree frog is not a 'pet' in the same sense that a dog or cat is. They are shy, secretive, and prefer to be left alone or in the company of their own kind. Handling, petting, and other direct contact from humans stresses them out.

Remember: just because you cannot touch or interact with the frog the way you can with your hamster or kitten doesn't mean that you can't enjoy it for what it is: a colourful and graceful animal that provides enjoyment to its owner in a less direct way.

Chapter 6) Red-Eyed Tree Frog Housing

The size of the enclosure depends on the number of red-eyed tree frogs it will contain. A single frog requires a 10-gallon tall tank, with an extra 10 gallons for each additional animal. When it comes to room, more is definitely better. If an enclosure is too small, the frogs may feel too confined and become stressed.

The enclosure needs to be tall, as red-eyed tree frogs are arboreal and will need branches and foliage to climb. A secure screen lid is recommended because it will provide much-needed ventilation while the glass walls will lock in the required amount of humidity.

The plants you choose should be washed before you put them in the tank and of a variety that is not harmful to the frog. All unpackaged decorations such as rocks should also be washed and rinsed thoroughly to remove dust and any traces of cleaning agents that the shop may have used.

Opinion is divided amongst red-eyed tree frog keepers on whether or not moss is a suitable cage decoration or substrate. There is always a risk that the frog could accidentally swallow the moss when trying to seize prey, creating a life-threatening bowel impaction.

The shop I go to uses ZooMed terrarium moss because it comes in big chunks that the frog can't consume as easily.

For Dexter, I use coco fibre and have never encountered any issues. I have seen forum comments to the effect that this material can irritate the frog during its first week in the new cage because it is loose enough to stick to their feet, but regular misting seems to take the 'edge' off. Some keepers use leaf litter over the substrate to minimise the sticky effect.

Humidity

Red-eyed tree frogs require adequate humidity. I keep Dexter's cage between 70 and 80%. It's a bit of a balancing act: higher humidity levels can cause respiratory infections, but lower ranges can cause the frog to experience dehydration. Some keepers recommend covering most of the screen lid with plastic or glass if humidity levels fall too low.

There are different humidity and temperature gauges on the market, but the closed probe type appears to be the most accurate. It can also be easily repositioned in different sections of the enclosure to compare levels.

Some frog keepers have found that heat lamps can 'burn down' humidity levels. If this happens and heat remains necessary, try switching to a ceramic heat emitter (CHE), which does not adversely affect humidity levels. I use one of these for Dexter in the winter.

One frog keeper I know uses a ZooMed HygroTherm™ to control the CHE: the device allows her to program both daytime and night time temps and supports successful simulation of nocturnal temperature drops.

Temperature

The optimum temperature range for red-eyed tree frogs is between 60-85°F. One breeder I know says that his pets do better with daytime temperatures of 78°F and 75-76°F at night.

There are two recommended ways for keeping enclosure temperatures at the preferred range.

The first is to control the ambient temperature of the room where the frog cage is located. This method works best if the room doesn't experience marked fluctuations in temperature due to seasonal changes. Otherwise go with the second option, which is directly warming or cooling the enclosure itself.

If temperatures fall too low, the frog's metabolism will slow down, stressing them to the point that they stop eating and can develop illnesses.

To add needed warmth, add an under-tank heater (UTH) to one side of the enclosure's bottom. If this doesn't provide adequate heat, place low-wattage incandescent bulbs outside the cage or use a low-wattage ceramic heat element that fits into a normal light fixture. Make sure that the bulb or element is not too close to the top.

It's important to remember that heat lamps can cause an enclosure to dry out, so regular misting will be necessary. Just be careful not to let the cool water hit the bulb, as it could shatter.

Keeping the frogs cool is a problem in warmer climates and during the height of summer. Keep the cage out of direct sunlight, close the blinds, and if the room is not air-conditioned, open the windows, use small fans to blow cooler air around, and mist the enclosure with cool water from time to time.

Water

Red-eyed tree frogs need constant access to clean water. At night, they hydrate themselves by finding their water bowl and submerging their backsides.

Make sure that the water has all traces of chlorine and chloramine removed before the frogs are exposed to it. Bottled water is the best and safest option, but tap water that has been left in a bucket or other container for 24-48 hours (the longer the better) will also be safe, as the chlorine will evaporate from it. Tap water can also be treated with products that dechlorinate aquarium water.

Whichever method you choose, be sure that the water is fully dechlorinated before you use it in the frog's enclosure, as chlorine will kill frogs.

Because frogs defecate and urinate in water, change the contents of their bowl or other water source frequently.

Plants

Aside from a tall tank and a steady supply of clean water, the best thing you can give your red-eyed tree frog is a lot of climbing material. Fake plants are the favoured option because they are easy to clean, don't carry unwanted parasites, and don't require the expensive lighting setups that some live plants do.

In Dexter's enclosure I keep a few Exo Terra Philodendrons as well as some real ones. The overlapping leaves provide him with a protected resting place, and when the time comes to find him a mate, the leaves can be positioned over water bowls to stimulate breeding.

When shopping for plastic plants, inspect them carefully for any sharp edges such as uncovered wires. The plants need to suit the frog's size too: most cheap artificial ones are fine for smaller frogs, but if your red-eyed tree frog is larger, find plants with leaf supports and wrapped wire stems.

After bringing them home, wash them thoroughly to remove dirt and dust. If you notice that dye bleeds out of the plant during the cleaning, don't use it: the dye can be absorbed through the frog's skin and cause potentially fatal complications.

Some frog keepers use outdoor branches in their pets' cages. If you do, treat the wood carefully to prevent pests and harmful substances from entering the enclosure.

Simulating the frog's natural environment eases the stress of being caged and helps them acclimate faster, which is important with wild-caught animals. Since these frogs love to climb and hide, broad-leafed plants such as Phildodendron and *Epipremnum aureum* are great choices if you want to provide them with live foliage. The latter plant is actually a vine and will quickly grow to cover the cage background.

35

When using live plants in your frog's enclosure, choose non-toxic varieties that are compatible with the animal's required living conditions. Then do the following:

- Remove the plants from the soil you bought them in and wash them thoroughly

- Replant them in soil that is free of pesticides, fertilizers, and other potentially harmful chemicals

- Let them grow in the new soil for at least a month and a half before adding them to the frog's tank. This allows all toxins remaining in the plant stems to gradually leave it.

When the plants are ready to be placed in the cage, set them up in their original pots or use a natural substrate piled 2-3" (51-76mm) deep. If the plant has roots requiring deeper soil, bank the substrate on one side of tank using a sturdy piece of cork bark.

If the enclosure contains a lot of live plants, it's a good idea to add drainage under the substrate. Stones are fine as long as they're not small enough for the frog to accidentally swallow.

Lighting

When it comes to lighting, I use a 5% UVB and give Dexter a light cycle of approximately twelve hours on and twelve hours off. You can use an appliance timer or do it manually, which is the option I use.

LED light systems are recommended because they don't affect (burn away) the humidity in the enclosure and the effect they produce is both pleasing to the eye and natural. Red-eyed tree frogs also hate bright lights and prolonged exposure can stress them out.

Aerosols and Sprays

Tree frogs can be killed by aerosol products such as hairspray, perfumes, disinfectants, and some types of pesticides. They absorb the airborne chemicals through their skin, so do not keep their enclosures in areas where aerosols of any kind are used.

Chapter 7) Feeding Your Red-Eyed Tree Frog

In the wild, red-eyed tree frogs will eat a variety of prey: crickets moths, flies, and even other frogs.

Crickets are a staple diet for most pet amphibians, and red-eyed tree frogs are no exception. For added nutrition, always gut-load the crickets beforehand. I feed my store-bought crickets fish flakes, oats, bran, dried cereal, and lettuce.

Gut loading, means, I quote from Wikipedia:"

Gut loading is the process by which an animal's prey is raised and fed nutritious foods with the intention of passing those nutrients to the animal for which the prey is intended. This term is used most often in reference to the preparation of insects, such as crickets and mealworms, or mice, which are used as food for reptile pets. Insects that are raised commercially for the pet trade are themselves of little nutritional value. By providing the prey animals with a high quality diet immediately prior to feeding, they become a more nutritious meal for the predator.[1]

Gut loading can be accomplished by providing fruits, vegetables, and cereals or a nutritionally complete manufactured diet. Several commercial products are available and are fortified specifically for gut loading. These products often include varying combinations of carbohydrates, fats, proteins, vitamins, minerals, and dietary fibre.

Gut loading is considered most important if the primary source of nutrition is from insects, especially crickets. Because crickets are lower in nutritional value than other common insects fed, such as mealworms and wax worms. Larval insects contain more protein and digestible energy than adult insects. In addition, when gut loading larva they will gain the nutrients needed to pupate quickly and therefore will not keep as long.

Gut loading is considered less important when animals such as mice are used as prey. This is because of the large amount of digestible energy and other nutrients a mammal contains in its tissues. It is also a less common practice when rodents are fed, because it is usually preferred to feed pre-killed prey from the store to protect the predator from being bitten.

Gut loading is designed to increase the nutrition of the prey's body and to fill the digestive tract of the prey with nutrients. As the term suggests, gut loading is usually looked upon as a way to get essential nutrients into a reptile via the ingestion of the digestive tract of the prey. The two methods of nutrient uptake are important due to the ability of the prey to process nutrients into a digestible form for the predator. For example, most prey can digest complex carbohydrates into other forms of nutritional energy, which the predator can use. However, gut loading nutrients like calcium do not have to be digested by they prey before its death in order to be available to the predator. Source: www.wikipedia.org

You can help to keep your frog healthy by 'loading' your crickets beforehand. This "gut loading" is done to ensure that the crickets being fed to your tree frog are full of vitamins that the frog needs to remain healthy.

Load up crickets by feeding them 24 hours before they go into the frog's enclosure. A variety of commercial cricket diets are available, but they're not recommended due to rich content, so you can feed the crickets with fish food, vegetable peelings or cereal type foods.

As a treat you can provide your frogs with wax worms, which are very high in fat so offer them sparingly. If wax worms are it's main food source, your frog will quickly become overweight, which can lead to serious health problems.

Offer food daily even if they don't eat as regularly. Healthy adult frogs will eat up to three crickets a day. Make sure that the prey items are no wider than the distance between their eyes: anything larger could cause a dangerous internal impaction (Impaction is a reason why you should never feed your frog mealworms, which have a shell). I feed my frogs ¾" crickets without complications.

When a new frog is brought home, they may refuse food due to stress. If that happens, don't panic: red-eyed tree frogs can go up to two weeks without eating and not suffer any lasting effects. Just leave them alone and continue to offer food.

Supplements

Dust the crickets with a high-quality vitamin and calcium powder. These are available from most specialty pet shops and online. I found the following 'recipe' on a frog forum and so far it has worked very well:

- Calcium without D3: every other feeding

- Calcium with D3: 2-3 times a month

- Multivitamins: 2-3 times a month

When I dust Dexter's crickets, I put them in a bowl. This will ensure that they don't lose the nutritious coating and that they're easier for him to catch. Many hobbyists only offer food in bowls to prevent their frogs from accidentally consuming substrate and other non-edible materials when hunting prey.

Chapter 8) Breeding Red-Eyed Tree Frogs

Mating Habits in the Wild

Red-eyed tree frogs begin to breed when the rainy season sets in, which is during the months of October and March.

To attract a mate, male frogs perch on the branches and vines over ponds and freshly created puddles and call out to all females in the vicinity. The sound, which resembled a single or double-noted 'cluck', issues around every ten seconds. As they call, the males quiver and even jump from branch to branch, raising themselves up onto all fours to make themselves appear bigger and more formidable.

If one male approaches another one's territory, a wrestling match will promptly occur. It's a fast and furious scuffle in which the males will try to climb on top of one another and pin each other into submission.

When female frogs hear the noise and emerge to see the males in territorial combat, their interest is usually piqued and they come out into the open. Once she steps into view, both males abandon each other and rush to be the first to climb onto her back. Then they fight to see who gets to hold the position.

The male who wins the contest will grasp the female tightly, his forelimbs over hers. Once the male is securely on her back (a position known as the arboreal oviposition or amplexus), the female slips into the pool or pond and takes water into her bladder. Then she will climb out onto a leaf or other piece of foliage that hangs over the water and lay a clutch of eggs. The average clutch contains around fifty eggs, although there have been reports of clutches as small as eleven and large as 158.

As she releases them, water issues from her bladder, preventing the eggs from drying out. Female red-eyed tree frogs can lay up to four clutches a night, but she has to fill her bladder back up with water between each clutch.

As the tadpoles develop, they begin wriggling about, until finally they rupture the membrane that envelops them and fall into the water, a process that takes six to ten days. The newly emerged youngsters search for food in the pool and finish the process of metamorphosis within forty to eighty days.

Breeding in Captivity

Because it is possible to artificially manipulate temperatures and wet-dry cycles, hobbyists can technically breed their red-eyed tree frogs at any time of the year.

Having said that, try to avoid the colder winter months, as it is not conducive to rearing tadpoles. Red-eyed tree frogs also tend to be a little slower and eat less during the winter. Spring, with its rising temperatures and barometric instability, is an ideal time.

Like many amphibians, breeding red-eyed tree frogs in captivity requires careful environmental manipulation. Once you have a healthy pair, complete the following steps:

- Start by cutting back on how often you mist the terrarium. Two light sprays per week will be sufficient

- Reduce the temperature by 5 degrees Fahrenheit.

- Frogs may not eat as much during this time, so offer food in smaller quantities, all the while monitoring them carefully to ensure that they remain in good health.

- After a month, return the terrarium to normal temperatures, mist heavily at least twice a day, and resume the regular feeding schedule.

- Males who are ready to breed will develop nuptial pads and start calling for a mate. Females who have been well fed and kept in proper condition will swell with eggs.

- If the females look especially plump and males are calling more frequently, move frogs to a rain chamber.

Creating 'Rain Chambers'

In the wild, red-eyed tree frogs breed during or following heavy rains. To replicate these wet conditions in captivity, it is necessary to create a rain chamber.

A rain chamber can be made from any container that's waterproof. A breeder I know uses a large aquarium, but you can even use a plastic bin. Construct a water section in the chamber by gluing a piece of glass into place at approximately the one-third mark in the tank's length. The rest of the tank floor can be covered with gravel or another substrate for the frogs to climb onto when they want to get out of the 'rainy section'.

Connect a spray bar to a pump and position it at the top of the enclosure. Make sure that at least 2" (52mm) of water covers the pump, and plug it into an electrical timer (if you have one). When the pump is switched on, water drops descend into the water section of the cage, simulating a rainstorm, and if a timer is applied, it can 'rain' for a few hours each night. Add an aquarium heater with a built-in thermostat set to around 80 degrees F.

Place several broad-leaved plants in the water for egg laying. Anthurium, Philodendron, and Spathyphylum are good choices. Do not use potted plants because their soil can contaminate the water. Experienced breeders also recommend adding some floating wood such as cork bark in the water area so the frogs can climb out if they fall in.

Competition Between Males to Encourage Breeding

Competition between males can encourage breeding, so try having a male to female ratio of at least 2:1.

Introduce the males to the rain chamber a few days before you add the females. If at all possible, move the frogs just before a thunderstorm is set to break out; it has been suggested that barometric pressure changes play a role in successfully breeding red-eyed tree frogs.

Mating Period

While the frogs are in the rain chamber, change a portion of the water daily to avoid the health problems associated with stagnant water. Feed the animals continually, removing all faeces and uneaten prey afterwards.

Watch carefully for signs of breeding. If nothing appears to be happening after two weeks, return the frogs to their enclosure, feed them a lot, and then attempt to breed them again.

If you spot an egg clutch (red-eyed tree frog eggs are a greenish colour with a clear gelatinous outer coat), remove it and place it carefully in a clean container with both land and water sections. If the eggs were laid on a plant leaf, remove the entire leaf and carefully hang it a few inches above the water.

44

The eggs need an ambient temperature of 74-78 degrees Fahrenheit to properly incubate in. Too low or too high may eventually kill the developing embryos.

Hatching the Eggs

Five to eleven days after they have been laid, the eggs will hatch and slide off the plant or leaf where they are perched and fall into the water.

The tadpoles tend to remain motionless on the bottom of the tank for a while after hatching. When they start to show signs of activity, feed them finely crumbled fish flakes and partially change the water daily to avoid stagnation and prevent build-up of harmful chemicals. Keep the water temperature between 74 and 80 degrees Fahrenheit.

Caring for the Babies

If their water temperature remains in the vicinity of 75 degrees F, most tadpoles complete their metamorphosis into froglets within 40-80 days. Once they develop their front arms, they can climb glass using their toe pads, so keep a screen top on their tank and give them a piece of floating cork bark to climb onto.

When they become terrestrial, they are a greenish brown colour with wide pupils and yellow irises. The elliptical pupils and bright red irises come about three weeks afterwards.

Once they can climb out of the water on their own, move the froglets to a simple enclosure with moist paper towel on the bottom, a water bowl and some plants for humidity and hiding purposes. It is important to keep them moist because they desiccate easily, but too much humidity can result in bloating and death, so monitor the froglets regularly and adjust the airflow when necessary.

Keep up to twenty froglets in a 10-gallon aquarium for the first month. As they get bigger, separate them according to size, so that the bigger ones don't steal all the food from the smaller ones. In terms of food, they will eagerly consume flightless fruit flies and pinhead crickets. Lightly coat each insect in high-quality nutritional supplements.

Depending on how quickly they grow, young red-eyed tree frogs can mature sexually in one year, but de Vosjoli recommends that they not be bred until they are at least a year and a half old, when they are able to cope with the attendant stresses.

Chapter 9) Medical Issues

Prevention is the best course of action when dealing with frogs. Keep their enclosures clean, with proper lighting, air circulation, and temperature, and make clean water available at all times. Dead plant material and uneaten prey should be removed as soon as you notice either, as bacteria and fungus can result.

Stress

Frogs can get really stressed when they are transported, so when moving them from one location to another becomes necessary, do it as quickly as possible and avoid handling them. Scared frogs can and do jump out of their owner's hand, sometimes injuring themselves in the process.

Transporting can be made easier on frogs by breaking them up into groups of two to three, and placing each group into a clean, plastic container. Include small bunches of sphagnum moss that has been treated in chlorine-free water.

If they are being conveyed by car, do NOT place the containers on the floor, where heat from the transmission can harm them. Buy a Styrofoam cooler or container in advance and place the frog container(s) inside, leaving the top off so that they can breathe.

Once you reach your destination, leave the frogs in their enclosure and do not disturb them except to check them on arrival. They will be hypersensitive after the trip and stress-related illness could set in. Wait a few days before interacting with them once more.

Oodinium

Oodinium is a common disease among red-eyed tree frogs. It manifests in the form of white or grey spots all over the animal's skin.

This condition is normally the result of dirty cage conditions, but it can also be caused by red leg disease (see below).

If caught in time, oodinium can be treated by putting the frog in distilled water and thoroughly cleaning the habitat.

Red Leg Disease

If your frog starts acting lethargically, take a closer look at its belly and inner thighs. If the skin there is noticeably red, the frog probably has red leg disease.

Red leg disease is typically caused by the parasite *Aeromonas hydrophyla*. It appears as reddened skin on the belly and underside of the frog's thighs, and afflicted frogs tend to be apathetic and slow. Because this disease can be deadly, isolate any sick frogs immediately.

To prevent onset, keep your red-eyed tree frog's enclosure clean and remove any dead prey items regularly. If red-leg has already set in, bathe the animal in clean water and sulfamethiazine. Then re-house it in a clean 'hospital' container. If the marks remain even after bathing, see a vet.

How the disease is treated depends on what caused it. If the frog is a newly imported, wild-caught specimen, dry packing can cause abrasions and redden the skin. If this is the case, put the frog in a pristine cage for at least three or four days.

Red leg can often be treated by bathing the frog in sulfamethiazine daily for two weeks (Use 15ml of sulfamethiazine for every 10 litres of water). If it does not improve after the first week of treatment, consult your veterinarian, as sometimes they will respond to antibiotics such as tetracycline.

Metabolic Bone Disease

If your frog's limbs become distorted, making it difficult for the animal to move, the probable culprit is metabolic bone disease.

The main cause is low levels of dietary calcium, causing the frog to leach the calcium it needs from its bones.

To prevent this disorder, add a light dusting of calcium powder to its prey two or three times a week. If the frog is already showing evidence of metabolic bone disease, contact a veterinarian experienced in amphibian care.

Hypervitaminosis

Hypervitaminosis is rarely reported among captive-bred tree frogs, but it does occur. If red-eyed tree frogs receive excessive levels of Vitamin D3 and calcium, they may suffer kidney damage, which manifests as edema. According to de Vosjoli et al, experts suspect that hypervitaminosis is to blame for calcium deposits on the internal organs and metabolic bone disease.

Reported symptoms include weight loss, lethargy, abdominal swelling, frequent urination, dehydration, constipation, and thickened and yellowing urates. If your frog manifests these symptoms, cut down on the supplements and contact a vet.

Dehydration

Under adverse conditions red-eyed tree frogs can become severely dehydrated. This often happens when a frog escapes and remains at large for a while, or if the water in their enclosure dries out. The experienced hobbyists on frogforum.net recommended the following treatment to a member whose recaptured frog was extremely dehydrated, and it apparently worked!

- Purchase unflavoured pedialyte and prepare a bath with 1 oz of pedialyte for every 10 oz of lukewarm, dechlorinated water.

- Place enough of the mixture into a clean container to cover the frog up to the chin. Any deeper and the animal could drown, so be careful.

- Leave the frog in the bath for twenty minutes or more. The electrolytes in the pedialyte will help it rehydrate and provide it with a badly needed energy boost.

Obesity

When overfed, tree frogs can become obese and experience health problems that shorten their lives. If your frog starts to get so plump that it cannot move around easily, cut back on the amount of food you give it and, if possible, move it into a larger enclosure to encourage activity.

Internal Parasites

If a frog's faeces look normal but it is abnormally thin, it may have nematodes, or internal parasites. Have a faecal exam conducted by a veterinarian, who can also prescribe medication such as Panacur. If the faeces are bloody or runny, flagellate protozoans may be to blame. Have a vet do a faecal exam and prescribe metronidazole, an antibiotic used to treat these parasites.

Clouded Eyes

Clouded eyes can signify a number of illnesses: immune system failure, eye injury, or toxin absorption. Move the frog to a simple hospital container and see a vet about prescribing enrofloxacin (Baytril), an antibiotic.

Water Edema

Bloated red-eyed tree frogs can be suffering from kidney disease, especially if the bloating is in the limbs. This condition is rarely curable, but it can be prevented by keeping the frog's water clean at all times so that it does not absorb its waste from the container.

Finding an Amphibian Vet

New and inexperienced red-eyed tree frog owners (as well as those with a really sick animal on their hands) should consult a veterinarian who specialises in amphibians. They may not be easy to find in some areas, but a good place to start is the website for the Association of Reptile and Amphibian Veterinarians (www.arav.org).

ARAV has members worldwide and a searchable database. If you do not find a vet in your area, call or e-mail them, as there may be new members that have not been indexed yet.

Colleges and universities where veterinary medicine is studied are also good resources for locating amphibian vets.

If a local veterinary practice does have 'exotic' vets on staff, ask what kind of training and continuing education they have undertaken. Do they subscribe to the Journal of Small Exotic Animal Medicine? Are they members of ARAV? Do they attend reptile and amphibian veterinary conferences or belong to any herpetology societies?

It may take a while, but once you find a qualified and experienced vet, you will be set for emergencies.

Feeding an Ill Frog

To orally administer medicine or water to your red-eyed tree frog, cut a wedge from a plastic container and slide it gently between the frog's jaws to pry them open. If a frog is refusing to eat, its mouth can be opened using the same method and a pre-killed cricket inserted. Most times, the frog will swallow the cricket once it is released.

Chapter 10) Other Frog Pets

Keeping red-eyed tree frogs can (and usually does!) lead to an interest in other frog species. It happened to me.

The frogs covered in this section are hardy and easy to keep, which is why you can find them in most pet shops, unless local regulations dictate otherwise.

Green Tree Frog

Green Tree Frog.
Photo by Robert Baldwin

The green tree frog (Latin name Hyla cinerea) is a staple in pet stores that carry amphibians.

Those offered for sale in the North American pet trade tend to be native to the southeastern areas of the United States, namely Florida, Arkansas, South Carolina, and the southern regions of Georgia.

Small and simple yet attractive with their cool green skin and cream-coloured underside, the green tree frog is often the first pet in an amphibian enthusiast's collection. Their average lifespan is anywhere between two and five years, and owning them tends to open the gate to a serious amphibian-keeping hobby.

The green tree frog is one of the easier frogs to maintain in captivity, as it is disease-resistant and eats a variety of insect-based foods. They should be misted once a day with chlorine-free water: I mist my two green tree frogs in the morning to prevent bacterial build-up.

Green tree frogs range in colour from a light lime green to a dark olive shade with brown undertones. They reach an average size of 2" (51mm), with males being slightly smaller than females.

When males attain sexual maturity, they will call out for mates in a manner that's either endearing or annoying, depending on whether or not you're trying to sleep.

Housing

One adult green tree frog needs a 10-gallon enclosure, with an extra 5 gallons for each additional frog.

The daytime temperature in the basking area beneath the light should be 78 - 80 degrees F, and night time temps should be 70 - 75 degrees F. Humidity should be 30 to 50%.

Diet

In terms of feeding, I give my two frogs three crickets every other day. Green tree frogs will eat flies, mosquitoes, and other small insects. One study suggests that they choose prey items not by size, but by activity levels.

Breeding

The green tree frog breeds from March to October in the southern areas of its native habitat and from April to September in northern regions.

Large groups of males will gather near wet areas and call out to attract females. During amplexus male green tree frogs sit on the female's back and tickle her to encourage egg laying.

The female will lay up to 400 eggs in shallow water with aquatic plants. The males will then fertilize the eggs by discharging sperm onto them. The tadpoles hatch in about a week and become frogs in two months.

Green tree frogs are reportedly not easy to breed in captivity, but success has been reported from those who set their pets up in a secure greenhouse with an artificial pond and aquatic plants.

White's Tree Frog

The White's tree frog (Litoria caerulea) originates from Australia and New Guinea. Like the green tree frog, they are frequently found in pet stores because they are hardy, long-lived (average lifespan is 15 years) and easy to take care of.

Adult frogs are 4-5" (102 – 127mm) in length, with the females being slightly larger.

White's Tree Frog.
Photo by Robert Baldwin

White's tree frogs are on the slow side- unless they're hungry. Then they lunge for the nearest cricket with a speed that belies their sometimes-dumpy appearance (Their nickname is the 'dumpy tree frog'). A friend of mine has two, and she swears that they know when she's going to the cricket pen. They stare at her through the glass walls of their enclosure, mapping her every move with keen interest.

Although I prefer not to touch my frogs, I know a lot of White's tree frog owners who handle theirs. When I visited the Reptile Store in Hamilton, Ontario, Canada, the manager took out one of their specimens, and the frog seemed to enjoy climbing on his arms and sitting on his hand.

If the frog doesn't appear to be stressed by the contact, holding them occasionally is fine, but the handler should wash thoroughly with soap and water afterwards, as White's tree frogs have a toxin in their skin that can cause irritation if washing doesn't follow a handling session.

Change their water daily, as clean water is a major factor in keeping them healthy.

Housing

White's tree frogs should be kept in a 10-gallon tank at the minimum, with an emphasis on height. Avoid gravel, pebbles, and other substrate that can't be safely ingested, as these frogs, like their red-eyed cousins, can be a bit careless when snatching up prey. They do best at temperatures ranging between 70 to 85 degrees F and a relative humidity of 50% or more.

Diet

White's tree frogs will eat crickets, mealworms, hornworms, and, according to some owners I've spoken to, the odd pinky mouse. Do not overfeed them, as they are prone to obesity and all its attendant illnesses.

Breeding

Male White's tree frogs have a wrinkled vocal sac on their throat region, while the females have a smooth white throat. The females have a white throat.

Breeding takes place in the rainy season, with preferred locations being wet sites such as drainage systems, water tanks, or semi-permanent water systems.

A clutch contains from 150 to 300 eggs. Once fertilized, the eggs sink to the bottom, with hatching taking place about 24-36 hours later. If conditions are favourable, metamorphosis can occur in two to three weeks.

Cuban Tree Frog

The Cuban tree frog (Osteopilus septentrionalis) is native to Cuba, but as a result of individuals escaping from captivity, it is considered a highly invasive species in Florida, Georgia, the Hawaiian island of Oahu, and the Caribbean Islands. The species is now banned from sale in Hawaii, and importation of a Cuban tree frog is punishable by a maximum fine of $25,000 (£14,700) and a year in jail.

Cuban Tree Frog.
Photo by Robert Baldwin

Cuban tree frogs are becoming more common in the pet trade, with healthy individuals living 5-10 years.

At 3 to 5 ½" (76 – 140mm) in size, it is the largest North American tree frog, and varies in colour from greenish brown to grey-green and even cream, with individuals being able to rapidly change shades. The Cuban tree frog's back is wart-pebbled, like a toad's, and it has large black eyes.

Cuban tree frogs are not recommended for beginners, especially children, as they secrete toxic mucus that can burn the eyes or trigger an allergic / asthmatic reaction.

Housing

Keep a single adult Cuban tree frog in a 15-20 gallon tank, with foliage to climb on and a place to swim in. A friend who has been keeping them for years fills a pet water dish with fresh water and includes a couple of rocks in case the frog needs to climb out quickly. Maintain a basking spot of 80-85 F during the day using an overhead bulb of 60-80 watts, depending on room temperature.

Diet

Cuban tree frogs will eat anything they can fit into their mouths, and may turn to cannibalism if other sources of food, such as crickets, are not available. There have even been reports of these frogs climbing utility poles to forage for food (usually hatchling birds) and causing costly power outages by short-circuiting the switches!

Feed adult frogs three times a week and juveniles daily. Each feeding session should consist of as much as the animal will eat in 15-20 minutes. Some Cuban tree frog owners give their pets the occasional pinkie mouse: this is fine as long as pinkies are an infrequent treat. Otherwise the frog may accumulate fat in its system and cause fatty liver disease to occur.

Breeding

Cuban tree frogs are sexually dimorphic, with females being larger than males. Mature males develop black nuptial pads on their thumbs, which help the males get a secure hold during mating.

Although Cuban tree frogs can breed year round, they do it most commonly during the wet season, between May and October. Partial egg clutches can yield 100-1,000 eggs, while a full clutch can total up to 4,000.

Eggs tend to hatch in less than 30 hours and the tadpoles can fully develop in one month.

Pac-Man Frog

Pac-man frogs (Ceratophrys ornata) come in several different

colours and are also known as ornate horned frogs , Argentine horned frogs and simply horned frogs. Under optimal conditions, they can live approximately 15 years.

Pac-man frogs must hold a record for being the laziest predators: they will burrow into their substrate and sit there with their eyes barely visible above the surface. Make sure that they have a substrate they can dig

Albino Pac-man Frog. Photo by Robert Baldwin

into. Damp (but not soaking wet) coco fibre is great. Some pac-man frog owners give their pets water bowls, while others say that it is not necessary if the substrate is kept moist.

Beware: pac-man frogs have teeth, and large specimens will draw blood if they catch your fingers. As a result, handle them only when absolutely necessary.

One more thing to keep in mind: if you think your pet is dead, it might not be. If their cage conditions are too dry or food is scarce, they will encase themselves in a thick outer skin to prevent further moisture loss and look dead. But once rehydrated, pac-man frogs will shed and eat this outer skin.

Housing

Adult pac-man frogs can be kept in 10-20 gallon enclosures. Normal room temperatures of 65-85 degrees F are fine. Since these frogs are fond of hiding spots, they do well in enclosures that include live or fake plants. If they cool down too much and dry out, pac-man frogs can enter a brumation state and refuse food, so adjust temperatures and cage conditions accordingly.

Diet

Every pac-man frog owner I've spoken goes on and on about their voracious appetite. Give them crickets and other insects, but offer an occasional treat of worms, small fish, and even small mice. Avoid mealworms and super worms due to their hard outer shell. If the frog starts to look too large, cut back on the feeding, as they will gorge themselves.

Breeding

Female pac-man frogs grow larger than males, and do not make noise. Males are quite vocal, often after being sprayed with water!

Anyone interested in breeding their adult pair needs to keep them in cool conditions (approximately 70 degrees Fahrenheit) for two months. (They will probably not eat during this period.) Then put them together in a shallow tank of water, with floating plants. If they mate, eggs are usually laid within three or four days. Remove the adults promptly, to prevent them from consuming the eggs.

When the tadpoles hatch, separate them or keep them in an enclosure with ample hiding opportunities, as they will readily eat each other. After about a month, they will begin transforming into froglets.

African Dwarf Frogs

As their name suggests, African dwarf frogs (Hymenochirus boettgeri) are small, only reaching around 1.5" (38mm) inches in length.

They live an average of five years, although some individuals have enjoyed a 15-year

Figure 1African Dwarf Frogs. Photo from author's collection

lifespan in captivity. Try to avoid handling them, as they can't survive longer than 20 minutes out of water.

Housing

Each frog should be allotted two gallons of water each, but keep the depth no more than 18" (457mm) or the frog will have a difficult time reaching the surface to breathe.

Substrate is not necessary, but if you decide to use it for aesthetic appeal, stick to aquarium gravel. Anything larger might trap or injure the frog and smaller material could be accidentally ingested.

Give them plenty of hiding spots, as they have a lot of natural predators in their native habitat and they feel more secure with retreats available.

In terms of temperature, 75-80 degrees F is preferable. Africa dwarf frogs don't have special lighting requirements, but keep the room where their tank is located dark overnight to maintain a day-night cycle and slow down algae growth.

Diet

African dwarf frogs eat bloodworms, brine shrimp, krill, or glass worms. Many pet stores offer special frog and tadpole pellets for this species. Once a week they will shed their skins and eat the empty skin afterwards, as it's surprisingly loaded with nutrients.

Thanks to their easy care regimen, African dwarf frogs can be found in novelty and 'eco-earth' shops as well as pet stores.

Breeding

Male African dwarf frogs are smaller and more slender than females, and have small white or pink glands behind their armpits. When they 'sing' to females, the sound resembles a quiet humming!

When conditions are right a male will call out and perform a mating dance. If he finds a receptive female he will grasp her from behind. She will swim to the surface and lay her eggs, scattering them around while the male fertilises them.

The eggs will hatch 24-36 hours later, with the tadpoles metamorphosing into froglets approximately six weeks later.

Tomato Frogs

Tomato Frog. Photo by Robert Baldwin

The tomato frog (Dyscophus antongilii) is one of the most colourful frog species. Their backs range in shade from orangey-red to bright red with cream-yellow undersides.

Males rarely attain more than 3" (76mm) in size, while females can get as big as 5" (127mm). Females are also more brightly coloured.

Until the end of the 1980s this species was actively harvested for the pet trade. It has since been included in CITES Appendix I, and its capture and commerce are presently forbidden.

Current conservation actions include a dedicated breeding habitat within Maroantsetra in Madagascar. Named "Tomato Frog Village", it protects one of the most prominent frog populations.

When threatened, tomato frogs 'play dead'. If that doesn't work, they may 'balloon', or puff themselves up with air to increase their size. As a last resort, they will secrete a white substance that coats the intruder's teeth / fingers. This substance is a toxin that is not harmful to humans.

Housing

In terms of cage requirements, tomato frogs like high humidity. Spray their habitat with water at least once a day, and use a substrate that retains moisture well.

Maintain an ambient daytime temperature of 75 degrees F: night time temperatures can safely be allowed to reach 65-74 degrees. It might be a good idea to keep one side of the enclosure warmer (80 degrees for juveniles, 85 for adults) in case the frog needs additional heat.

These frogs love to burrow, so give them at least 2 ½" (64mm) of substrate to dig into. Common substrates include coco fibre, chemical-free potting soil, or damp moss.

Diet

Tomato frogs are greedy eaters: anything that moves and can fit in their mouths is fair game. Crickets, mealworms, locusts, wax worms, and small cockroaches are popular fare. They should be fed three or four times a week, with calcium or multivitamin powder being sprinkled on their prey over other feeding.

Be warned: they quickly recognize routine when it comes to food, and owners who maintain a regular feeding schedule will soon find these frogs eagerly anticipating them.

Breeding

The breeding season for tomato frogs begins in March, after the rainy season. Adults gather in ponds and marshes and the males call up to 60 times in a row, with each episode lasting up to two minutes!

The female will lay up to 1,500 eggs that metamorphose into froglets approximately 45 days after hatching.

African Bullfrog (Pixie Frog)

The African bullfrog (Pyxicephalus adsperus), otherwise known as the pixie frog, is one of South Africa's biggest frogs. They have pebbled olive-green skin and thick bodies with wide heads. Males can be distinguished by their massive size (up to 10" / 254mm and weighing 4lbs / 1.8 kgs) and yellow throats, while females have cream-coloured throats and rarely get larger than 6" (152mm) long and 2 lbs / 0.2kgs in weight. According to one exotic pet website, they can live up to 35 years!

Housing

Because they can get so big, pixie frogs need decent-sized enclosures. A 20-gallon aquarium will suit an adult male. Give them fresh water every day and clean their bowl just as often, as they're notorious for defecating in it.

Pixie frogs prefer a deeper substrate so they can dig into it. One frog keeper I know uses chemical-free potting soil, while another prefers his own concoction of sphagnum moss and sand. (Avoid loose moss, which can be accidentally ingested.)

They require warmer temperatures (80-83 degrees F seems to be average) and high humidity, the latter of which can be attained via daily misting with chlorine-free water.

Diet

Like pac-man frogs, these huge amphibians love to eat. They actually have tooth-like projections on their lower jaws for grabbing and holding larger prey items. (One pixie frog in a zoo supposedly ate seventeen young cobras!) Their regular diet consists of large insects, worms, and even small rodents. Because they're not opposed to eating other amphibians, it's a good idea to keep them separate unless you're breeding.

Breeding

The easiest way to determine the sex of a pixie frog is by listening, as males will call out during the mating season. Males also grow larger, have broader heads than the female, and have yellow or orange chests. Females tend to have cream-coloured undersides and can retain a dorsal stripe as they mature.

Wild pixie frogs mate after the onset of heavy rains. Temporary pools are quickly taken over by the males, who will call and fight other males to attract a mate. During amplexus up to 4,000 eggs can be spawned, which are then guarded by the males. Once spawned, eggs will hatch within 48 hours and metamorphosis into froglets takes approximately 2 to 4 weeks, depending on site conditions.

Resources

Below is a list of popular web forums dedicated to frog enthusiasts. All links are valid at the time of publication.

- Frog Forum http://www.frogforum.net/: Active community that has been discussing frogs and toads since 2008. Includes photo galleries, blogs, and subsections on popular species and their care.

- Frogs.org.au http://frogs.org.au/community/: Australian forum that allows members to tap into the combined knowledge of experienced frog keepers and breeders.

- Dart Frog Forums http://www.dartfrogforums.com/: Although dart frogs are the primary focus, this forum also has practical advice about tree frogs.

- Reptile Forums http://www.reptileforums.co.uk/forums/: UK-based forum that has an active and insightful amphibians section

Further Reading

Bartlett, R.D. and Patricia Bartlett. *Red-Eyed Tree Frogs and Leaf Frogs*. Hauppauge: Barron's Educational Series, Inc., 2000

De Vosjoli, Phillippe, Robert Mailloux, and Drew Ready. *Popular Tree Frogs*. Irvine: Advanced Vivarium Systems, 2005

Duellman,WE. *The Hylid Frogs of Middle America.* Lawrence: Museum of Natural History, University of Kansas, 1970

Grenard, Steve. *Frogs and Toads: Your Happy Healthy Pet.* Hoboken: Howell Book House, 2007

Mara, W.P. *Breeding and Keeping Frogs and Toads*. Neptune: TFH Publications, 1994

Wright, Kevin *Amphibian Medicine and Captive Husbandry* Malabar: Krieger Publishing Company, 2001

Glossary

Advertisement call: The mating call of male red-eyed tree frogs

Amphibian: Cold-blooded vertebrate animals that spend part of their lives in water. The word means 'double life.'

Amplexus: The mating position of red-eyed tree frogs. The male climbs atop the female and grasps her with his front legs.

Anura: The order of animals in the class Amphibia. It consists of more than 5,000 species, including frogs and toads.

Archaeobatrachia: A suborder of the order Anura. It contains various primitive frogs and toads such as Hochstetter's frog (*Leiopelma hochstetteri*)

Army: A group of frogs.

Chorus: A large group of frogs calling or singing

Chytridiomycosis: A fungus that effects the permeability of a frog's skin. It is lethal to most frogs, but some can be asymptomatic and carry the fungus to others.

CITES – The Convention on International Trade in Endangered Species of wild fauna and flora. Trading in CITES-listed species is illegal.

Cold-blooded: An animal that cannot regulate its own body temperature, forcing it to exchange heat with its environment. The scientific term is 'ectothermic'.

Detritus: Decaying plant and animal matter that collects at the bottom of a body of water.

Dorsal: Upper side of the frog, or its back.

Ecosystem: A community of organisms that live, feed, and reproduce in the same physical environment.

Habitat: The location where a frog species originates.

Herbivore: An animal that eats plants.

Herpetology: The study of reptiles and amphibians.

Insectivore: An animal that eats insects.

Invasive Species: A species of frog that is not native to a certain area and has negative effects on the environment.

Metamorphosis: The process by which tadpoles turn into froglets.

Nictitating membrane: A frog's transparent inner eyelid.

Nuptial Pads: Thumb pads present on mature male frogs.

Ranavirus: An amphibian disease that causes tadpoles to die.

Spawn: Frog eggs.

Tadpole: The pre-froglet stage of the frog life cycle. Tadpoles have gills for absorbing oxygen from the water and a tail for swimming

Toe Pads: Disc-shaped sticky areas on the toes of red-eyed tree frogs

Tympanum: A frog's eardrum.

Vernal Pools: Temporary seasonal ponds usually caused by rains

Published by IMB Publishing 2014

Lightning Source UK Ltd.
Milton Keynes UK
UKOW06f1451300714

236029UK00007B/35/P